Sexual Ethics

SEXUAL ETHICS IN ISLAM AND IN THE WESTERN WORLD

Murtada Mutahhari

TRANSLATED
Muhammad Khurshid Ali

Islamic Centre of England

British Library Cataloguing-in-Publication Data
A catalogue record for this book is available from the
British Library.

ISBN: 978-1-904063-46-9 (pbk)

© ISLAMIC CENTRE OF ENGLAND, 2011
This edition first published in 2011

Distributed by ICAS Press, 133 High Road, London NW10 2SW

Islamic Centre of England
140 Maida Vale, London, W9 1QB
www.ic-el.com

Contents

Introduction

Ayatollah Murtada Mutahhari was born in 1919 to a clerical family in the village of Fariman near the holy city of Mashhad. As a child, he attended the traditional *maktabkhaneh*, but when he reached the age of twelve, he began his basic training in the Islamic sciences at the seminary in Mashhad. In 1937, he left for Qum to commence his advanced training in Islamic sciences in the seminary there. During his fifteen-year stay in Qum, he attended the lectures of Grand Ayatollah Muhammad Husayn Burujerdi on jurisprudence and the principles of Islamic jurisprudence; the lectures of Ayatollah Ruhullah Khomeini on Mulla Sadra's philosophy, mysticism, ethics, and principles of jurisprudence; and the lectures of 'Allamah Sayyid Muhammad Husayn Tabataba'i on philosophy, the *Elahiyyat* of Avicenna, and other subjects. Before Grand Ayatollah Boroujerdi moved to Qum, Mutahhari used to visit the Grand Ayatollah's hometown of Burujerd to attend his lectures. He also attended the mystical and ethical discussions of Ayatollah Haj Mirza Ali Aqa Shirazi and was influenced by him spiritually. His other teachers included Ayatollah Sayyid Muhammad Hujjat (principles of Islamic jurisprudence) and Ayatollah Sayyid Muhammad Muhaqqeq Damad (jurisprudence).

In addition to his studies, during his sojourn in Qum, Mutahhari was involved in socio-political activities. For instance, he was in touch with the Fada'iyan-e Islam group headed by the charismatic young cleric Navab Safavi. In 1952,

Mutahhari moved to Tehran and continued his scholarly
activities at the Marvi Seminary. Three years later he began
teaching at Tehran University in the School of Divinity and
Islamic Sciences.

Mutahhari's serious involvement in politics began in 1963
with the popular 15th of Khurdad uprising which was brutally
suppressed by the Shah's regime. He was detained and
imprisoned numerous times afterwards. Mutahhari was also
the religious guide of Hay'at-ha-ye Mu'talefe-ye Islami, a
group formed under the guidance of Ayatollah Khomeini.
Later, Mutahhari played a pivotal role, along with a number
of other activists, in establishing the Husayniyyeh-e Ershad.
After a dispute with the leading figures of the Husayniyyeh-e
Ershad, he decided to offer his lectures elsewhere in Tehran,
including at the al-Javad and Ark mosques. In the months
leading to the 1979 Islamic Revolution, Mutahhari was among
the closest confidants and advisers of Ayatollah Khomeini,
who appointed him to form the Revolutionary Council.
Almost three months after the victory of the revolution,
Mutahhari was assassinated by a shadowy anti-clerical group
called Furqan that staged a campaign of terror and
assassination against leading clerics after the revolution.

Mutahhari was one of the most outstanding Muslim
thinkers in our era who was able to formulate novel and
impressive theories while remaining rooted in authentic
Islamic traditions. He was committed to principles of belief in
Shi'a Islam but fully informed of modern social and
philosophical theories and the ideas of modern Muslim
intellectuals. Consequently he was able to influence the
intellectual currents in Iran. He was a critic of not only
Marxist thought, but also western secular liberalism. He
responded to many critiques of religion emerging from the
Eastern Bloc and the West. However, he also criticized
superstitious beliefs and un-Islamic conduct among Muslims.

Mutahhari is one of the most prolific writers and Islamic
scholars of our era. To date, more than ninety of his works on

various fields of Islamic scholarship have been published. Most of these works were originally delivered as lectures during his life and later compiled as books and articles after his assassination. Some of these works are his personal handwritten notes which he himself did not have the opportunity to publish. Hence, it can be said that some of the published works were bound to have been published with a degree of haste. If his productive life had not been so tragically cut short by the bullets fired on that spring night in Tehran three decades ago, these works would have been fully edited and the content and the form would have been different. At any rate, despite all this, what Ayatollah Khomeini said about his works stands true even today: 'All the works of Martyr Mutahhari are beneficial and valuable without exception.'

It can be said that despite his vast encyclopaedic knowledge of fields such as jurisprudence, Qur'anic sciences, and *hadith*, Mutahhari should be remembered as a theologian-philosopher. His philosophical works and his commentary on classical philosophical books clearly show his mastery of Islamic philosophy. But we must note that he is most impressive when he provides convincing theological apologetics for the principles of faith in Islam. He maintained this theological approach in his writings on society as well. A review of his works shows his keen interest in social issues, and the issues of the youth and Shi'a academicians, clerics, and thinkers. Mutahhari was active in improving the affairs of religion and reforming the clerical organisation and the institution of the *marja'iyyah*. He was one of the contributors to the famous compilation of articles called *Marja'iyyat va Rawhaniyyat* which was published in 1961 after the death of Grand Ayatollah Burujerdi. Mutahhari also fought against the chauvinistic propaganda of the Shah's time that attempted to create a rift between Iranians and their Islamic roots. His seminal work, *Khadamat-e Mutaqabel-e Islam va Iran (Mutual Contributions Between Islam and Iran)* was a collection of articles that he published in a pseudo-feminist Iranian magazine called *Zan-e Ruz*. At a time when a wave of pseudo-feminism was being propagated by the Pahlavi regime, Mutahhari did not have any compunction about writing in a magazine that was hated by religious groups as the preeminent pseudo-feminist rag of its day. Mutahhari's concern with women's issues resulted in the publication of two very important works: *Nezam-e Huquq-e Zan dar Islam* (*The System of Women's Rights in Islam*) and *Mas'aleh-ye Hijab* (*The Issue of Hijab*).

Mutahhari's theological writings aimed at debunking Marxism and atheism and destroying the sway that they held over the Iranian intellectuals at the time. *'Elal-e Girayesh beh Maddigari* (*The Causes of Attraction to Materialism*) was a pathology of the roots of materialism in Iranian society. His philosophical works include a commentary on *Usul-e Falsafeh va Ravesh-e Realism* (*Principles of Philosophy and the Method of Realism*), a voluminous work written by his teacher, 'Allamah Tabataba'i; *Sharh bar Manzumeh* (*A Commentary on Haj Mulla Hadi Sabzevari's Manzumeh*); and *Dars-ha-ye Elahiyyat-e Shifa* (*Discourses on the Elahiyyat Section of [Avicenna's] Shifa*). Such works attempt to explicate the philosophical dimension of Islamic thought for researchers and those interested in the rational sciences. His insightful and meticulous commentary on the statements attributed to Prophet Muhammad (S) and Imam Ali (A) appears respectively in *Sayri dar Sireh-ye Nabavi* (*A Glance at the Prophet's Life*) and *Sayri dar Nahj al-Balaghah* (*A Glance at Nahj al-Balaghah*). Both works show a great mind at work, displaying his commendable efforts at understanding the vast wisdom of the Infallibles (A).

Mutahhari was also a leading reformist of his time. He was not a reformer who would do away with the traditions, fall into the trap of eclecticism, or become overwhelmed and consumed by a faddish new trend. Mutahhari masterfully utilised all the Islamic sciences; Islamic teachings; and philosophical, mystical and ideological challenges to enrich religious knowledge and provide solutions for some of the social and intellectual challenges of his time. In this effort, the most important characteristic of his reformism was that he attempted to present a clear and enlightened understanding of Islam in a bid to end malicious misinterpretations of Islam.

This book, *Akhlaq-e Jinsi dar Islam va Jahan-e Gharb* (*Sexual Ethics in Islam and in the Western World*), contains a series of articles that Mutahhari published in *Maktab-e Islam*, the leading religious journal in pre-revolutionary Iran. During Mutahhari's lifetime, a rogue publisher compiled these articles and published them as a small pamphlet without securing his permission. Of course, this happened much to the chagrin of Mutahhari because the articles need to be edited, updated and revised before they appeared in a book form. Moreover, Mutahhari had plans to include them in his *Nezam-e Huquq-e Zan dar Islam* and was planning to publish them himself. Despite all this, he did not prevent the publication of the book. All this also explains why the work does not contain a preface by the author and why the tone of the book is for general audiences. The discussions are meant to remove the misunderstandings promoted among the intellectuals, university students, and young men and women by feminists and secular writers who enjoyed the full backing of the Pahlavi regime. Although Mutahhari intended to respond to the prevailing misunderstandings of Islamic beliefs on the subject, he also clarifies principles on gender, sexuality, and women's rights. Mutahhari masterfully explains why the Islamic approach to marriage and morals differs from traditional negative moralizations as well as the negative sexual attitudes that, for centuries, had affected credulous people, leading to misconceptions about sexuality and irrational attitudes towards women – particularly among some ancient peoples and some Western modernists. Mutahhari clearly explains the Islamic perspective on human sexual relations and their boundaries. He explains that the

Islamic approach has well-known guidelines which lead neither to sexual deprivation and frustration, nor to repressed or inhibited sexual desire. He demonstrates that, from the Islamic point of view, sexual desire is not only compatible with human intellectuality or spirituality, but is also part of the nature and temperament of the prophets. Quoting various traditions, he shows that the prophet of Islam and the pious Imams all explicitly demonstrated love and regard for their wives. At the same time, they strongly disapproved of celibacy or monasticism.

In clarifying the Islamic perspective, Mutahhari engages in a critique of Marxist and Western views on sexuality – views rooted in the Western philosophical tradition. He is staunchly opposed to liberating human sexuality from the traditional moral restraints and social prohibitions, and believes that doing so is bound to lead mankind towards self-destruction. According to Mutahhari, the only school of thought still capable of guiding humanity towards a moderate sexual lifestyle is Islam.

It goes without saying that a brief overview of Western philosophers cannot serve as a full critique of Western philosophy – especially since Western philosophers obviously hold a diversity of opinions on any subject, including this one. Mutahhari himself does not claim that all Western philosophers held Russell's view. However, for the sake of argument, it is justifiable to choose representatives of a certain intellectual current and, on this basis, critique their views. What is important here is that the principles which Mutahhari critiques – such as individual freedom and its conflict with social rights, physical and spiritual happiness, the innate nature of a human being and human instinct (especially with regards to the sex drive), sexual freedom and limitations, and religious views on sexuality – are openly discussed in the works of such thinkers. Mutahhari relied on the existing translations in Farsi (and perhaps Arabic, which he had mastered as an Islamic scholar) to become familiar with the views of these Western philosophers and provide a robust Islamic critique of Western approach to sexuality.

The style of argumentation in this book was popular during Mutahhari's era, and some of what he was discussing was controversial at that time. However, the topics Mutahhari chose are still relevant. He skilfully applied the clarity that he is renowned for in the numerous useful discussions on subjects which can be sensitive even in academic circles. I hope and pray that the readers, especially the younger generation, will benefit from this book.

S. KHALIL TOUSSI
London, 2 March 2011

1

Islam and Traditional Sexual Ethics

For Muslims, the institution of marriage – which is based on the mutuality of natural interest and cordiality between spouses – represents a sublime manifestation of the Divine Will and Purpose. This is discernible in the Qur'anic verse cited below:

> And one of His signs is that He created mates for you, that you may find rest in them, and He envisaged between you love and compassion . . . . (Qur'an, 30:21)

According to Islamic tradition *(sunnah),* marriage is essential. Celibacy is regarded as a malevolent condition fraught with evils.

The Islamic approach to marriage and morals differs from negative traditional moralizations. Surprisingly enough, certain traditional moralists regarded sexuality as something wicked. They viewed sexual intercourse – even with one's legal spouse – as impure, evil, undesirable, destructive, and a characteristic of the guilty and fallen.

Still more surprising is the Western notion that the traditional world viewed sex as evil. The famous Western philosopher, Bertrand Russell, is no exception in this regard. In his book *Marriage and Morals,* he generalizes:

> . . . anti-sexual elements, however, existed side by side with the others from a very early time, and in the end, wherever Christianity and Buddhism prevailed, these elements won a complete victory over their opposites. Westermarck gives many instances of what he calls 'the

1

curious notion that there is something impure and sinful in marriage, as in sexual relations generally.'

> In the most diverse parts of the world, quite remote from any Christian or Buddhist influence, there have been orders of priests and priestesses vowed to celibacy. Among the Jews the sect of the Essenes considered all sexual intercourse impure. This view seems to have gained ground in antiquity....There was indeed a generalized tendency towards asceticism in the Roman Empire. Epicureanism nearly died out and stoicism replaced it among cultivated Greeks and Romans....The neo-Platonists were almost as ascetic as the Christians. From Persia the doctrine that matter is evil spread to the West, and brought with it the belief that all sexual intercourse is impure. This is, though not in an extreme form, the view of the Churc h....[1]

Throughout the centuries, negative sexual attitudes continued to affect masses of credulous people and inspired repugnance towards sex. Some psychoanalysts attribute the high incidence of psychosomatic disorders and spiritual ailments largely or solely to the widespread prevalence of deeply ingrained negative sexuality.

What could have caused these misconceptions about sexuality? Why would people have denied themselves the natural satisfaction and the psychosomatic well being associated with healthy and desirable sex? Why should people lead their lives so as to virtually condemn an essentially wholesome part of their lives? These are some of the complex questions for which thinking people have yet to provide meaningful and convincing answers. Yet we all know that there could be many different reasons for, and causes of, aversion to human sexuality.

Apparently, these reasons included prejudicial thinking about sexual desire and intercourse. This prejudice was carried to the extreme among the Christians as they organized their churches and the clergy.

Due to the celibacy of Jesus Christ, they considered marriage a pollution of chastity and piety for saints and preachers. Accordingly, Popes are always chosen from among unmarried priests. In fact, all the members of the Catholic clergy are bound by their oaths of celibacy intended to help them remain virtuous.

Bertrand Russell quotes W. E. H. Lecky as saying:

> Two or three beautiful descriptions of this institution [marriage] have been culled out of the immense mass of the patristic writings; but in general, it would be difficult to conceive anything more coarse or repulsive than the manner in which they regarded it... The object of the ascetic was to attract men to a life of virginity, and as a necessary consequence, marriage was treated as an inferior state... To 'cut down by the axe of Virginity the wood of Marriage' was in the energetic language of St Jerome, the end of the saint....[2]

The Church approves of marriage for purpose of human procreation. However, the need to propagate the human species was not enough to lift the stigma of impurity from any sexual act. They also conceded the necessity of marriage in order to eliminate fornication. Again, to quote Bertrand Russell:

> Christianity, and more particularly St Paul, introduced an entirely novel view of marriage that it existed not primarily for the procreation of children, but to prevent the sin of fornication.[3]

The Catholic Church regards marriage as sacrosanct and binding until death. Accordingly, dissolution of a marriage or divorce is not permitted. The prohibition of divorce may have something to do with a possible desire to atone for the Original Sin, due to which Adam and Eve were expelled from Paradise in an unmarried state.

Irrational attitudes towards women prevailed among some of the ancient peoples. These included the notion that a woman was not a complete human being, for her situation as a creature might well lie somewhere between a human being and an animal. Also, she was devoid of an articulate spirit, so that she could never enter Heaven! Similar other superstitions were rampant in the past.

Fortunately, however, the aforementioned beliefs and notions were not universally carried to the extreme. Women's natural limitations, as identified and evaluated in the past, were not encroached upon. The impact of traditional thinking did not go beyond the cultivation of a sense of male pride and inculcation of a sense of female inferiority through generations.

Belief in the inherent wickedness of sexual desire and intercourse distressed men and women absolutely and equally in spiritual terms. Moreover, it caused a rather demoralizing conflict between the natural, instinctive urges and religious or sectarian beliefs about wickedness of carnal desire and sexual intercourse.

A conflict arose between genuine natural desires and the socially induced aversion to their fulfilment This caused spiritual ailments and unhappiness. The problem assumed extraordinary proportions, insomuch as it became the subject of intensive investigations by psychologists and psycho-analysts.

In the above context, the revolutionary logic of Islam can be of extraordinary interest. Islam does not give the slightest indication that sexual desire is evil in and of itself, or that it is necessarily fraught with evil consequences. On the contrary, Islam aims at regulating human sexuality in a most humane manner.

From the Islamic perspective, human sexual relations are limited only by the genuine interests of the present society, or the posterity. Therefore, the Islamic approach follows well known guidelines, leading neither to sexual deprivation and frustration, nor to any repression or inhibition. It is a pity that scholars, like Bertrand Russell, who has evaluated

Christian and Buddhist morals, have refrained from specifically commenting on Islamic ethics.

In his book *Marriage and Morals*, Bertrand Russell mentions Islam in passing:

> Great religious leaders, with the exception of Mohammad – and Confucius, if he can be called religious – have in general been very indifferent to social and political considerations, and have sought rather to perfect the soul by meditation, discipline and self-denial.[4]

Nonetheless, from the Islamic point of view, sexual desire is compatible with human intellectuality and spirituality. It is also part of the nature and temperament of the prophets. According to one narration *(hadith)*, love and affection for women were characteristics of the moral conduct of the prophets (من أخلاق الأنبياء حب النساء).

There are several other narrations indicating the prophetic regard for women. According to some, the Prophet of Islam and the pious Imams too have all explicitly demonstrated their love and regard for their wives and the womenfolk. At the same time, they have strongly disapproved of celibacy or monasticism.

One of the companions of the Holy Prophet, Uthman bin Mazoon, devoted himself to Allah's worship to such an extent that he fasted almost every day and kept regular nightly prayer vigils. His wife brought the matter to the attention of the Prophet, who reacted with visible annoyance, proceeded at once to the companion, and said:

> O Uthman! Know that Allah has not deputed me to encourage any monastic life. My shari'ah laws are meant for enhancing and facilitating human accomplishment of their natural lives. I offer my prayers, keep fast and maintain my conjugal relations. Accordingly, to follow me in Islam means conforming to the traditions laid down by me, which include the requirement that men

and women should marry and live together harmoniously.

The Islamic position – as explained above – makes it clear that human sexuality in and of itself neither represents any inherent wickedness or evil. Furthermore, it clarifies the traditional perspective that human sexuality is inherently evil – the perspective that the Western world adopted as religious morality evolved there. Now, the Western world has taken a 180-degree turn and reversed its extreme traditional morals to another extreme.

At present, the Western world believes in lifting traditional moral restraints and respecting and freeing sexual desires and involvements. In fact, many Westerners now favour sexual permissiveness. They contend that their inherited morality carries no more than a religious connotation. They claim that today's new morals are based on not only philosophical but also scientific grounds.

Unfortunately, the negative Western views of sexuality – both the traditional and the recently evolved ones – have penetrated the moral fabric of our society too, despite all the erstwhile difficulty of international communication. Now with improved means of communication and regular international contacts, these modernistic Western morals are virtually flooding our society, as will be explained later on herein.

Notes

[1] Bertrand Russell, *Marriage and Morals* (London: George Allen and Unwin Ltd., 1976), 31-32.
[2] Ibid., 39-40.
[3] Ibid., 35.
[4] Ibid.

2

Sexual Ethics as Conceived by Modern Thinkers

Sexual morals constitute an integral part of behavioural ethics applicable to human beings. Included in sexual ethics are some of the various social norms, personal habits and behavioural patterns which are associated directly with the sexual instinct. Some aspects of sexual ethics and practices include:

1. Female modesty;
2. Male sense of honour concerning female members of a household;
3. Female chastity;
4. A wife's faithfulness to her husband;
5. Female inclination to cover her private parts, or her aversion to exposing any bodily nakedness in public;
6. Prohibition of adultery;
7. Interdiction of any visual or physical intimacy with women other than one's legal wife or wives;
8. Prohibition of incest, or marriage between persons too closely related;
9. Avoidance of sexual intercourse with menstruating women;
10. Debarring pornography or obscenity;
11. Treating celibacy as either saintly or undesirable.

The sexual instinct is, by its very nature, quite extraordinary. Also, it is powerful in its manifestation.

Accordingly, sexual morals are the most important part of ethics.

In his book *Our Oriental Heritage,* Will Durant highlighted the fact that marrying and settling down was always considered to be one of the very important moral duties of human beings. He said that the natural human capability for procreation involved difficulties, not only at the time of marriage, but before and after that, as well.

The difficulties could be aggravated by the intensity and vehemence of the sexual instinct, as well as its aversion to moral and legal constraints. Further, it might even lead to deviation from its natural course. All these and more, as mentioned by Will Durant, meant extreme confusion and organisational disorders, if and when a society could not provide necessary and effective safeguards.[1]

Any academic and philosophical discussion of sexual morals must first consider their origins and evolution. For instance, it is necessary to know how the modesty and chastity of women have come to be safeguarded. The fact that men traditionally protect their women, as part of their own sense of honour, could be due to identifiable or specific reasons.

The male aptitude for possessiveness and protection of women may not necessarily be attributed to any inborn jealousy in men. For human jealousy has universally been considered a negative emotion. Has an exception been made in favour of jealousy so as to safeguard the husband-wife relationship? If so, why? If there are other reasons for men to protect the honour of their women, as if it were a question of their own honour, how can these be explained?

Likewise, the desires and social norms favouring clothing or covering of the female body, curbing sexual promiscuity, prohibiting marriage between persons too closely related and similar other moral and legal restraints must be explained. Their examination can be in terms of whether or not they are rooted in human nature, physiological or psychological.

Then one may ask whether sexual morals are linked to the natural requirements of gregarious living, or whether they are an inborn tendency, related to the natural process of human survival. Or could historical (rather than natural) causes have gradually affected and influenced human consciousness and behaviour?

If the source of human morality were entirely rooted in nature, it would be hard to explain how both the ancient aboriginals and today's isolated primitive tribes, living in the manner of their ancestors, were and are quite unlike civilized peoples.

The origins of and rationality behind sexual morality may be diverse, as can be the historical conditions of social evolution, with reference to human sexual ethics in particular. Nevertheless, the question relevant to us now is whether or not traditional morals still promote overall human progress under modern conditions.

Specifically, we must ask ourselves whether or not we must now safeguard the traditional sexual ethics or replace them by instituting new morals.

Will Durant does not trace human sexual morality to any natural origins. He attributes moral evolution to historical experience, even some occasional unhappy or cruel happenings in the past. He favours retaining the substance of traditional morals but allowing continued moral evolution in order to selectively practise the best without shortcomings.

Referring to morals concerning female virginity, modesty and bashfulness, Will Durant observes that traditional values and customs evidence a natural process of moral selection across the centuries. According to him, virginity and modesty are relative qualities linked with conditions of marriage and traceable to a past situation requiring purchase of, or bargaining for, wives.

Will Durant recognizes that the moral and social requirements of female chastity and modesty are of basic importance to any society, even if these qualities are sometimes capable of giving rise to psychosomatic and nervous disorders. Moreover, the relevant social regulations are essential for promoting a harmonious continuity in sexual relations in the context of marriage and family living.

Freud and his followers subscribed to a different view of sexual morals. They sought to dispense with traditional sexual morality, or to replace it with something altogether new. In the opinion of Freud and his followers, morals were based on limitations and prohibitions concerning human sexuality. They claimed that the limitations and prohibitions caused many human afflictions and gave rise to emotional disturbances, including subconscious fears and obsessions.

Basically similar arguments have been put forward by Bertrand Russell. He defends the position that nothing should be regarded as taboo. His views concerning marriage and morals are independent of any moral considerations, such as those of chastity, rectitude, modesty, any male sense of honour encompassing the female (which he suggests is actually jealousy), and others.

The proposed liberation of human sexuality from traditional moral restraints is tantamount to claiming that nothing ugly, bad or disgraceful can come out of this liberation. The impression is conveyed that nothing but the human intellect and its rationalization is being relied upon. The proposal concedes no more restraint on sex than any natural limitation of food intake!

Elsewhere, Bertrand Russell tried to answer the question as to whether or not he had any advice to give those who wanted to follow a correct and sensible path in matters of sex. He replied that the question of sexual morality should be examined analytically like any other problem. If, upon adequate examination, it was found that others would come to no harm from one's pursuing a certain manner of sexual conduct, we would have no reason to condemn any such individual rationalization and practice.

When asked whether the violation of female chastity

should be viewed as an exception to his contention that actions causing no harm or loss to others should not be condemned, he explained that loss of virginity could be due to an act between two individuals. However, if it was construed as a violation of the chastity of a virgin, there should be evidence to the same effect before it could be condemned as rape.

For the time being, we may refrain from a detailed examination of the question as to whether or not human traits like modesty or sexual chastity are rooted in Mother Nature, for the question is very broad in scope. One can hardly give a completely scientific answer. Assumptions, not even approximate ones, cannot be based on whatever has been indicated thereon so far, for those who base their opinions on assumptions often lack consensus.

For instance, human inclinations like sexual modesty are viewed differently by Freud, Will Durant and Bertrand Russell. The nature and content of their differences need not be detailed herein. Suffice it to mention that these writers seem to base their views on the assumption that human qualities like female modesty are not inborn or in any way specific to human nature. If so, their understanding of human characteristics shows what appears to be a disinclination to seek a correct justification.

Be that as it may, we can indeed make two assumptions regarding sexual habits and inclinations. Firstly, we may assume that sex-oriented behavioural qualities have no connection whatever with the innate nature of human beings. Secondly, we may suppose that the 'habits' are inculcated as part of other human practices and norms, under some kind of a social contract, designed to harmonize individual and social interests, as well as assure the peace and well being of mankind.

Let us now ask ourselves whether or not logic and reasoning demand intrinsic values and safeguards to assure complete psychological harmony and maximize human wellbeing and peace. We may further ask ourselves whether or not eliminating moral and social restraints and limits will be conducive towards achieving complete psychosomatic harmony of individuals and enhancing social welfare.

Then, we may well realize that logic and reasoning deem it advisable for us to oppose every customary practice and superstitious habit which implicitly treats human sexuality as unclean and pernicious. At the same time, we are likely to consider it necessary that we should refrain from promoting any unrestrained sexual freedom which causes widespread excesses, transgressions and agonies.

The supporters of the proposed new sexual liberty base their arguments on three premises:

1. Individual freedom should be ensured, as long as it does not interfere with other people's freedoms.
2. All inborn sexual desires and aptitudes should be freely nurtured and brought to fulfilment without any inhibition or restraint, since curbing or frustrating them leads to ego disorders.
3. Natural desires subside when fulfilled, and become insistent and excessive when subjected to any negative moral restraint or ill-conceived prohibition.

The sexual liberationists argue that emotional instability arises from discriminating among the natural instincts and desires, so that only part of these are satisfied while the others remain frustrated. So, they say, equal nurturing and development of all human inclinations is necessary for personal and societal well being.

Furthermore, they suggest that the only way to avoid constant preoccupation with sex is to lift all moral restraints and social prohibitions. They claim that liberation of the natural process of sexual fulfilment will also pre-empt the mischief, malice, and vengeance characteristic of a situation involving moral restrictions.

The foregoing arguments constitute the basis on which

the new sexual morality is proposed. God willing, we should be able to render these arguments untenable, through an adequate investigation and a thorough evaluation of the three basic premises mentioned above.

Notes

[1] Will Durant. *Our Oriental Heritage* (New York: Simon and Schuster, 1935).

3

The Proposed New Sexual Freedom

A critical analysis of the basic principles of the proposed new sexual freedom occurred in the preceding chapter. In this chapter, we will examine the salient features of the proposed new sexual liberation, especially its approach to reforming conventional morality. This will be conducive to a detailed analysis which is not likely to be thorough otherwise.

It should be recognised that there are people who are already convinced about these new ideas regarding sexual conduct. At the same time, it is worthwhile – even necessary – to discuss social problems, including those of sexual morality, from various angles. For the question of sexual ethics has received the attention of famous thinkers of our age. Above all, it is notable that many young people have uncritically accepted the proposed new approach to human sexuality. The views of well-known modern personalities are apparently taken to be infallible.

In our opinion, our esteemed readers must be made aware of the implications of our impressionable young people acquiring even rudimentary assimilations of novel Western ideas, including some with innocuous labels, such as *freedom* and *equality*. This is because we must know how we are applying our minds, to what purpose and towards what end. Will blind acceptance of ideas contribute to human progress?

Or else, is the Western intellectual and cultural penetration of our society too ill-informed and too ill-conceived a propaganda strategy that, if allowed to spread, will lead mankind towards self-destruction?

The above questions will be discussed herein, in a necessarily brief manner. A more elaborate discussion of the relevant issues can be found in the author's book, *Woman and Her Rights.*[1]

The reformers claim that traditional sexual morals no longer exist, or else are in the process of vanishing. They say that we no longer have any justification to continue holding the old morality since the causative factors and the original conditions have changed. The severity of this has occasionally been evidenced.

Furthermore, they point out that, aside from the changed or changing conditions, there have historically been events involving the old morality in an ignorant and cruel manner. They believe that past experiences were inconsistent with the concepts of freedom, justice and human dignity. So, for the sake of humanity and justice, they appeal that we must oppose all moral restraints on sex.

Opponents of the traditional sexual morals say that these old concepts gave rise to the following:

1. Male possessiveness of females;
2. Male jealousy;
3. Male concern over establishing the paternity of a child;
4. Asceticism and monasticism based on the assumed sinfulness and wickedness of human sexual relations;
5. Female sense of impurity arising from her menstruating nature;
6. Male abstinence from sexual relations with a menstruating female;
7. Women undergoing severe punishments at the hands of men throughout recorded history;
8. The economic dependence of women on men.

They claim that the above stems from the conventional sexual morality and is indicative of cruel and superstitious individual and social restraints applied under primitive conditions. They seek to replace these old values with modernistic permissiveness. For one thing, they point out that modern wives are not to be treated as chattels.

In the same vein, they proclaim that, today, contraceptives remove any need to forcibly ensure the paternity of a child through the old moral prescription of female chastity!

The supporters of the proposed new sexual freedom further affirm that the old ascetic and monastic orders and beliefs are dying out. Knowledge and sanitary means of personal hygiene are said to have freed women from harbouring any sense of pollution while menstruating. They are convinced that the days of male cruelty and oppression are gone forever.

They conclude that enslaving or mistreating women and making them utterly dependent on men are now things of the past, for women are regaining socio-economic freedom. Moreover, modern governments are gradually taking upon themselves the major socio-economic responsibilities of a husband and father, including maternal care and childcare. On the other hand, human jealousy is on the decline with the spread of modern sexual attitudes and behavioural norms. Accordingly, they suggest that we should no longer cling to the old moral system.

Sexual liberationists offer the foregoing criticism of the old morality as the basis of their proposed new morals. Of course, this is to be expected of those who oppose conventional morals.

Now, let us examine the proposed new morals. At the outset, we recognize that they revolve around casting away the traditional sexual restraints. Accordingly, they turn their attention first to the freedom of the individual to fulfil one's sexuality or bring about conditions of free sexual love.

In pursuit of sexual liberty, they affirm the unrestrained joys of not only premarital but even post-marital sexual experimentation. They point out that through inexpensive and rather safe means of contraception, sexual enjoyment can be diversified without necessarily involving any risk of pregnancy, legitimate or otherwise. Thus, they claim that married people can safely pursue their love affairs to their heart's content, by taking lovers or becoming a love object without necessarily undermining their marriage. Moreover, they imply that not only illegitimate pregnancies can be avoided, but a wife can chose to have a legitimate child without any moral concern about her extramarital affairs.

Any communism in sexual matters is obviously undesirable. Also, it is impracticable if the genetic need to ensure paternity of a child is to be ensured. Even those who propose the new sexual freedom seek to retain the legitimacy of a child and to safeguard paternity. After all, a father's blood relationship with his son and the son's filial obligation and affinity towards his father are always recognizable. This is the philosophy behind selection of a particular spouse and one's marital undertaking to voluntarily confine sexual relations to her or him. In fact, conventional morality highlights no greater need for married couples than to confine their sexual relations within their marriage.

Bertrand Russell's proposed new morals are cited below:

> Contraceptives have made parenthood voluntary and no longer a result of sexual intercourse. For various economic reasons . . . it seems likely that the father will have less importance in regard to the education and maintenance of children in the future than he has had in the past. There will therefore be no very cogent reason why a woman should choose as the father of her child the man whom she prefers as a lover or companion. It may become quite easily possible for women in the future, without any serious sacrifice of happiness, to select the fathers of their children by eugenic considerations, while allowing their private feelings free sway as regards ordinary sexual companionship. For men it would be still easier to select the mothers of their children for their desirability as parents. Those who hold, as I do, that sexual behaviour concerns the community solely in so far as children are involved,

must draw from this premise a twofold conclusion as regards the morality of the future. On the one hand, that love apart from children should be free, but on the other hand, that the procreation of children should be a matter far more regulated by moral considerations than it is at present.[2]

Bertrand Russell elaborates further as follows:

> When science becomes able to pronounce on this question [of eugenics] with more certainty than is possible at present, the moral sense of the community may come to be more exacting from a eugenic point of view. The men with the best heredity may come to be eagerly sought after as fathers, while other men, though they may be acceptable as lovers, may find themselves rejected when they aim at paternity . . . . [3]

Bertrand Russell's statements and proposals sometimes reflect a moral angle, too. For instance, he believes that traditional morality has been designed to cope with strong and potentially troublesome human emotions, such as jealousy, which he advises men and women to consciously overcome:

> In the system that I commend, men are freed, it is true, from the duty of sexual conjugal fidelity, but they have in exchange the duty of controlling jealousy. The good life cannot be lived without self-control, but it is better to control a restrictive and hostile emotion such as jealousy, rather than a generous and expansive emotion such as love. Conventional morality has erred, not in demanding self-control, but in demanding it in the wrong place.

Russell recommends the same self control that was prescribed by the ancient moralists. However, he envisages self-control not for the conventional reasons of ensuring self-respect and rectitude, but for completely overcoming jealousy. Contending that the ancients sought to unduly limit human sexuality, he advocates a jealousy-free attainment of human sexuality. He considers conventional morality – which provides for personal honour, individual modesty and self-respect – to be outmoded. He seems as if he would rather see husbands who do not get jealous over their wives' intimacy with other men and who are even grateful for the social permissiveness that allows extramarital relations with third persons.

At the same time, Russell says that children ought to be born to married couples only. He would like to ensure the use of contraception during premarital, extramarital or post-marital sexual relations. Furthermore, he recommends that:

> It is also by no means impossible that the jealousy of husbands should, by a new convention, adapt itself to the new situation, and arise only when wives propose to choose some other man as the father of their children. In the East, men have always tolerated liberties on the part of eunuchs which most European husbands would resent. They have tolerated them because they introduce no doubt as to paternity. The same kind of toleration might easily be extended to liberties accompanied by the use of contraceptives.[4]

The foregoing typifies a kind of reform of the extant social ethics, which in all probability would entail a never-ending process. No doubt, it would mean radical changes in other ethics too, including legal safeguards concerning female modesty, incest, pornography, homosexuality, abortion, sexual intercourse during menstruation, and so on. Some of these, like protecting female modesty and banning pornography, are sometimes upheld. Other questions, like homosexuality, have occasionally been treated outside the purview of sexual ethics in a clinical manner so that medical considerations – not necessarily moral restraints – can prevent any deviant behaviour!

The modernistic sexual ethics described above must be thoroughly examined before being accepted readily. In the present context, only the basic elements will be discussed and evaluated. Then, the philosophy underlying Islamic morals, which are quite distinctive from Western morality (traditional as well as modern), will be explained. This will highlight the Islamic position to the effect that the only school of thought still capable of guiding humanity through the distressingly unwholesome effects and untoward consequences of Western speculations concerning the dynamic philosophy of human living and sociological evolution is that of Islam. It is high time that West-oriented societies, with all their scientific and industrial advantages, realize their continuing need to turn Eastward in the process of their assimilating a salutary philosophy of life, as they have indeed done in their past epochs.

Notes

[1] Murtada Mutahhari, *Woman and Her Rights* (a translation of *Nezam-e Huquq-e Zan dar Islam*), trans. M. A. Ansari (Karachi: Islamic Seminary Publications, 1982). <http://www.al-islam.org/WomanRights/index.html>.

[2] Bertrand Russell, *Marriage and Morals*, 173-174.

[3] Ibid.

[4] Ibid., 194-195.

4

A Critical Examination of the Theoretical Basis of the Proposed New Sexual Freedom

In the preceding chapter, the salient features of the proposed new sexual morality have been discussed. Now, its basic principles will be evaluated. These are restated below:

1. Individual liberty should invariably be respected and protected, provided it does not conflict with that of others. In other words, an individual's liberty is limited by no other consideration than the liberty of another individual.

2. Human wellbeing lies in nurturing and fulfilling the individual's inborn aptitudes and desires. Interfering with these natural inclinations will lead to egotism and personality disturbances arising from sexual frustration in particular. The natural instincts and desires are bound to go awry if they are not fulfilled or satisfied.

3. Restraining natural instincts and desires tends to intensify cravings and inflame passions. Their uninhibited fulfilment allows for contentment, enabling a person to overcome any excessive preoccupation with a natural urge, such as the sexual one.

The three principles above concern human philosophy, development and psychology, respectively. They are put forward as justifications for what the new moralists consider to be the correct way, i.e. dispensing with conventional morals, restraints and limitations in order to ensure individual liberty to promote (rather than frustrate) sexual gratification.

First, let us examine the above principles on the basis of the statements and views of the supporters of the proposed new moral system. For none of them seem to have fully identified the principles underlying their contributions to the proposed new morality.

The principle of individual liberty is actually basic to the sociological realization of human rights. However, those who seek to promote the new concepts of morality evidently – and wrongly – assume that personalized sexual freedom has no social implications. This is because of their obvious assumption that when individuals are free to pursue their sexual interests, they are expected to observe no more than privacy, so as not to adversely affect other people's rights.

At the same time, they recommend safeguards in the interest of society, even to the limited extent of assuring paternity and care of children. According to their proposed new safeguards, a wife is to bear her husband's child only. Otherwise, she is free to pursue her sexual interests, using contraceptives, which not only prevent pregnancy, but enable her to ignore the time-honoured moral restraints of chastity and faithfulness, if she so desires.

In the above context, two implications concerning individual freedom require detailed examination. The first one arises from the modernistic contention that personal liberty should only be limited by the need to respect other people's individual liberties. The second implication refers to the claim as long as there are no concerns over paternity or the filial affinity of a child, sexual relations do not have any further connection with society, public life and social prerogatives.

Let us consider the philosophy behind individual liberty. The most essential aspect of personal freedom – and in one's entitlement to its protection – is the need to gradually evolve a harmonious and respectable manner of progressing one's individual life in order to enhance the higher faculties. Due emphasis on the aforesaid need is noticeably missing in several Western interpretations or applications of the concept of personal freedom. In any case, individual freedom should not lead to any sexual permissiveness, enabling one to pander to lusty impulses and self-centred desires. For any misuse of personal freedom should not be encouraged or respected by those who can (or ought to) realize its dire consequences.

It is misleading to say that everyone's personal liberty should be cherished as long others' entitlements are respected. For, aside from the need to avoid interpersonal conflict, every society must recognize that people's individual freedom ought to be limited due to the larger and higher interests of people themselves. Any continuing neglect of the aforementioned moral requirement can further aggravate the harm already done to the very basic concept of morality and the wrong done to the understanding of personal freedom in its own name!

Bertrand Russell was once asked as to whether or not he would consider himself bound to any particular system of morality. He replied in the affirmative and proceeded to explain his answer by giving a hypothetical example of how individual morality can be viewed in the social context. The scenario he mentioned was more or less as follows:

> Suppose Mr. X wants to do something which is useful to himself, but harmful to his neighbours. Then he carries out his intention, inconveniencing his neighbours. The neighbours decide among themselves to the effect: 'We don't like this situation and we should do something so that he doesn't take advantage of us.' Thus, the situation suggests a conflict of rights.

Bertrand Russell emphasized reasoning and intellectual judgment in the above case. Then he pointed out that morality did signify the need to harmonize the private and public aspects of individual behaviour.

From a practical viewpoint, the aforesaid case of new morality hardly suggests any Platonic utopia. Russell's interpretation of morality evidences no precedence of any inexorable values of life over intrinsically or potentially baneful things. There is no trace in his suggestions of anything that makes human beings subject themselves and their material interests to any higher intellectual or spiritual considerations.

On the contrary, he views morals involving comprehensive meaning and significance as taboo. The only thing he considers to be sacred or inviolable is accomplishing one's personal inclinations and desires without inhibition. The only restraint on any particular manifestation of individual freewill approved by him is its compatibility with that of other persons. Even so, he leaves the question unanswered as to what congenial power or faculty should be instrumental in keeping personal freedom within limits of reason, sanity and decency, and rendering it harmonious with that of others. Nevertheless, Bertrand Russell's scenario mentioned above is useful in attempting a possible reply to the question of individuals limiting each other's personal liberty. Accordingly, the scenario can be adapted as follows:

> Mr. X's neighbours can restrain or stop him from harming their interest, while serving his own. He is convinced that his neighbours in their own interest will mutually agree to prevent him. Accordingly, he is reconciled to the fact of his helplessness to do anything without coordinating his own interest with that of his neighbours.

The foregoing is illustrative of the sterility of Bertrand Russell's moral philosophy, based as it is on the crucial stipulation that an individual can (or ought to) serve his own interest and, at the same time, safeguard the rights and interests of the general public (which is impossible, considering that no norms of individual and group behaviour can be identical).

Evidently, certain hypothetical assumptions underlie the new morality proposed by Russell. For one thing, he implies that individuals and groups in a society can always manage to employ their benign powers envisaged under the proposed new morality. Secondly, he assumes that interpersonal and group unity and consensus are always readily forthcoming against individual transgressors. Then, he takes it for granted that an individual, who stands alone and weak, can nevertheless always decide to initiate any action against something of interest to a majority.

However, individual and collective powers of thinking and action can vary. People adversely affected by an individual transgression are seldom prepared to unite. Furthermore, one does not always decide to act against any majority interest, especially without confidence in one's own strength.

The ethics proposed by Bertrand Russell may be cogent enough to be recommended to weak members of a society. For the weak may be readily cowed down by the sheer force of the strong and influential whose rights they may dutifully respect. However, when it comes to actually preventing any transgression by the strong and powerful against the weak, the proposed ethics will probably fail to take effect.

For the strong may gang up against the weak. They may stifle any rare protest or overwhelm any sign of resistance from the weak. Even worse, the strong can always say that their behavioural philosophy is not against the new recommended ethics! In actual practice, they can even deem it unnecessary to harmonize their personal interests with those of the others.

Accordingly, Russell's moral philosophy may be construed as one of the most effective means of perpetuating the dictatorial concept of *might is right*. No doubt, Bertrand Russell devoted his active life towards advocating the cause of freedom, while defending the rights of the weak. Yet, ironically enough, his moral philosophy tended to consolidate vested interests and dictatorial tendencies in a society. This type of contradiction is often discernible in Western philosophizing, so that what is preached differs from what is practised.

The second implication concerns the private and public (or social) aspects of marriage and family life. No doubt, people who intend to marry are seeking individual happiness and mutual enjoyment of life. Now, two questions arise as to how best to promote their goal of achieving and maintaining a happy marital life. Firstly, one may ask whether this enjoyment is best accomplished within the privacy of a family itself. Alternatively, should any pursuit of sex-oriented happiness be extended beyond the privacy of family living to places of work, social encounters, downtown entertainment areas, or any milieu – outside a family – where people usually seek to fulfil sensuous or sensual pleasures?

Islam has recommended that a couple's mutual enjoyment be confined to the privacy of their family living, so that they remain fully oriented towards each other. Islam has determined that any sex-oriented pursuit of happiness and enjoyment in public is to be avoided. Accordingly, any vicarious satisfactions derived from a sexually permissive society, including female exhibitionism in public, are not allowed in Islam.

Western societies, which seem to blind some of us through our fascination, evidently favour the alternative proposition in the second question above. They have shifted the focus of attention to sex from the privacy of family living to its vicarious satisfaction in public. They do pay dearly for this moral lapse. Some of their thinkers express concern about deteriorating individual and societal morality in a sex-obsessed milieu. They are also stunned when they find how some communist societies have successfully taken sex out of the public arena and saved the youth in the process.

Enjoying life cannot be equated with lustful or sensual living.

Individual happiness does not lie in maximizing the pleasures of eating, sleeping and sex. On the other hand, one may suppose that human propensity to enjoy sex-like pleasures is instinctively limited, as in of animals, which could thereby lead to dissatisfaction.

However, this assumption can be wrong, since human search for physiological contentment is susceptible to be carried beyond married life and family living to the society at large.

However, persons of opposite sex whose souls, rather than bodies, have attracted each other can indeed be sincere in their mutual affection, after they agree to become husband and wife. Their marital happiness can extend beyond the passionate youth to mutually cherished companionship in ripe old age.

Likewise, it is conceivable that a man can discriminate the most intimate and satisfying relationship with his legitimate and faithful wife from any animal-like pleasures of the body, such as those obtainable from a prostitute. Accordingly, he would not want to replace what is most desirable and wholesome with what is sensuously pleasurable and conveniently transient.

Clearly, it is essential that activities involving human sexuality are limited to married couples in the privacy of their family living. For this purpose, it is necessary to safeguard the functional integrity and mutual compatibility of a family and its social milieu.

Marriage and family living are very significant functional aspects of a society. These institutions are responsible for the benefit of the posterity. The family upbringing of children determines the quality of successive generations. In this context, the individual and mutual capabilities of husbands and wives to raise children well is crucial. A father's concern for his offspring is bound to be conducive to a positive upbringing.

Human congeniality, in both individual and social contexts, is best developed in a harmonious family atmosphere. A child's exuberant spirit and natural temperament is substantially conditioned and trained by the parents.

When appealing to people's good sense and common interest, we invoke their affinity with the community they may belong to, or a sense of brotherhood. For that matter, we may even emphasize the brotherhood of mankind. The mutual devotion and faithfulness of pious believers is compared in the Holy Qur'an with the sincere regard that brothers have for each other.

Brotherhood among human beings does not come merely from any blood relationship or racial affinity. When we speak of the brotherhood of man, we suggest that the congeniality of two blood brothers can be reflected among individuals in a society. If brotherliness and affection which grow in a family are eliminated, it is doubtful whether people can really show genuine consideration for each other.

They say that in Europe, there is a considerable sense of justice, but fellow-feeling is very limited. Even real brothers, as well as fathers and sons, evidence very little affection for each other. This is quite in contrast to the general run of people and families in the East.

Why? The answer revolves around the fact that human love and sympathy are qualities which come from a wholesome upbringing of children by affectionate and united families. Evidently, families in Europe are no longer able to cherish these qualities effectively. The solidarity between husbands and wives, often noticeable in the East, is frequently missing in the West. A significant reason can be the fact that Westerners have come to believe in sex without love or inhibition. Sexual experimentation and diversification do not allow any specific interpersonal love to develop. They tend to be indiscriminate in seeking sexual enjoyment.

5

The Basic Need for the Humane Conditioning of Natural Instincts and Desires

The need to refine and condition the raw natural instincts and desires in a benign manner is basic. Harmonious personal growth is conducive to wholesome interaction with fellow men, which in turn leads to a salutary impact on the humanity at large.

Appropriate conditioning and training of an individual's natural potentialities brings about spiritual rewards, too. These include a spiritually balanced personal outlook and intellectual composure, necessary for any sound and beneficial endeavour. Psychosomatically balanced persons are emotionally stable and competent and can achieve social harmony and peace.

On the other hand, any unduly inhibited or imbalanced growth of an individual personality is quite undesirable. So are any adverse external influences or negative pressures. For negatively conditioned people become susceptible to causing excesses, untold miseries, and cruelties not only to themselves, but to others.

The traditional non-Islamic moralists regarded sex and love as if these were manifestations of an obnoxious evil to be shunned. In contrast, modernistic societies tend to consider free love as not only desirable but respectable. No doubt, the free love concept began to receive preferential treatment and encouragement for its worldwide growth.

Islamic morals can be properly understood with reference to the following points:

1. The compatibility of Islamic morals with the requirements of the natural growth of sexuality as one of inborn human instincts and potentialities;
2. The Islamic view on suppressing human lusts;
3. Modern sexual permissiveness as a major cause of sexual or sex-oriented aberrations or deviant behaviour, and as something which prevents the harmonious growth of the natural instincts and individual potentials;
4. Democratic attitudes towards sexual behaviour;
5. Morality as pertains to sexual ethics, as opposed to general ethical conduct in economics and politics;
6. Love and the forlorn condition in which it remains a longing;
7. Love and harmonious growth of human personality.

To begin with, it should be recognized that natural human instincts should be nurtured, and not suppressed. At the same time, it is necessary to conceptualize beyond any simplistic determination in terms of good and bad.

The Islamic approach takes into consideration the overall need to promote the healthy growth of the human personality as an a priori requirement, based on deductive logic. The premises recognized in Islam include the factual position that every constituent part of the human body has a specific purpose or function. The biological purposes and functions are sustained by a person's will to nurture them, even beyond the instinctive motivations. Accordingly, human volition, intellectual capabilities and similar other aspects of the spiritual nature must be enhanced too.

We could well imagine a situation where no traditional evolution of morality is allowed. This would mean that the inborn human potentialities are either harmoniously cultivated or prevented from such development. In any case, it stands to reason that human faculty to discern things and to comprehend the natural order of things would induce the necessary process of harmonization.

A hundred years ago, scholars and social scientists recognized the need for a psychosomatically balanced development of human personality. Societies of the time lacked a correct overall human perspective. There was a markedly deficient realization of the moral traditions. Negative tendencies affected all-around human development.

In fact, there has never been any doubt about promoting an all-around growth of human personality. This is implicit in the very word 'training', which has always been used to indicate human development.

Any correct and effective approach to the training of human beings must be aimed at overcoming tendencies leading to disturbances of personality and morbid conditions of disorder and indiscipline affecting the body, the mind and the spirit. A naturally harmonious and spiritually balanced plan for human growth should include the training of the sex instinct in particular.

In the above context, Islam offers the most appropriate guidance. This position is intended to be clarified and established in the discussion that follows.

At the outset, we must stipulate that any preconceived or ill-conceived notions concerning Islamic ethics must be avoided.

For instance, some people appear to harbour the notion that Islamic morality inhibits, rather than promotes, any free growth of human faculties. They wrongly believe that the Islamic teachings are irrelevant to refining and improving the natural human instincts.

In contrast, the Holy Quran is replete with emphases on human refinement, such as when it asserts that a conscientiously righteous person is one who has been able to refine, discipline and purify his natural instincts and desires (قَدْ أَفْلَحَ مَن زَكَّاهَا, 91:9).

This quotation further implies that the human conscience is liable to pollution. At the same time, it suggests that human beings can improve their individual conscientiousness by overcoming any polluted state. Above all, the Holy Qur'an considers a pollution-free conscience to be indispensable for attaining righteousness and happiness.

There can be no denying the intrinsic meaning and significance of the moral values taught by the Glorious Qur'an. The aforementioned teaching and its explanation pinpoints a conscientious approach to the problem of human refinement. No school of thought or moral procedure rules out human susceptibility to pollution of the conscience or psyche and the consequent need to purify and ameliorate the undesirable condition. The human psyche is vulnerable to prurient desires, moral aberrations and psychopathological disorders, just as the human body or organs are liable to disease.

An individual can feel within himself or herself the specific nature and extent of any of his or her physiological, psychological, or spiritual ailments. People do this far more completely and accurately with regard to themselves, than in respect to other persons (or for that matter, even in the case of any environmental pollution). Thus, it is possible and necessary to ensure righteousness and rectitude on an individual basis, through psychosomatically and spiritually harmonious personality development. The Holy Qur'an makes this point thoroughly clear.

There is another Qur'anic description of the raw, natural self of an untrained person (أَمَّارَةٌ بِالسُّوءِ, 12:53). According to this description, a person's untamed or inappropriately trained self is referred to as a *commander* of evil [thoughts and deeds]. Does it mean that a non-disciplined *self* can be wicked by nature, according to the Qur'an?

The reply to the abovementioned question cannot be positive. This is because, theoretically speaking, a human

being, if born malignant, cannot be expected to be amenable
to any training that seeks to metamorphose himself into
becoming naturally benign. On the contrary, the very
existence of naturally malignant beings deserves to be treated
as undesirable, since they are potentially harmful. They ought
to be prevented from growing and assuming menacing
proportions. Their malignant impact would need to be
curbed, even by occasionally eliminating them!

So, the correct answer is that there is no wickedness built
into the very nature of a human being. Only in particular
situations, and in specific circumstances, does an individual
become vulnerable to wickedness and, upon nurturing it,
develop a malignant disposition.

Any negative representation of man's basic nature as a
source of evil and wickedness is not implied in the Qur'anic
philosophy, as already indicated above.

Then, one may as well ask two more questions. Firstly,
what circumstances or causes lead human beings toward
becoming wicked and corrupt? Secondly, how can the
depraved and corrupt be rehabilitated?

Answers to the above questions require a comprehensive
and positive understanding of the relevant Qur'anic
teachings. For, they lie beyond any wrong and narrow
minded interpretations, such as arising from any literally
isolated or absolute or negative understanding of the
Qur'anic description of the human self as a *commander* of
evil. Actually, according to the Holy Qur'an, the self can be
not only a commander of evil, but a conscientious reprove
(النَّفْسِ اللَّوَّامَةِ, 75:2). Elsewhere, the Qur'an, refers to the self also
as an abode of human peace and excellence (النَّفْسُ الْمُطْمَئِنَّةُ,
89:27).

The Qur'anic descriptions of the *self* indicate that the
human nature can have different stages of growth and
manifestation. At one stage, it can be prone to mischief and
wickedness. When it perpetrates anything undesirable, it can

also ruefully blame itself. Above all, it is capable of attaining the highest stage of human excellence and composure, after which it is no longer vulnerable to doing anything bad or wicked.

Islam does not presuppose any inherent wickedness of human nature. So, it is at variance with the speculative philosophies and systems of human training evolved in India, or those enunciated by some ancient cynical philosophers. Furthermore, it differs from the teachings of Manes, of ancient Persia. The Islamic approach is distinct from that evolved in Christianity as well. The Islamic code of moral conduct does not evidently subscribe to any denial, or suppression, of human instincts, nor does it prescribe anything reminiscent of penal servitude in overcoming carnal desires.

The ancients might not have clearly realized that under specific circumstances (or in certain situations or at some stage of personal disciplining), human nature could go awry and become vulnerable to a wickedness or evil that is capable of assuming dangerous proportions. However, in modern times, now that a scientifically investigated basis of human personality development has been discovered, there can be no longer any doubt about the need to discipline one's own *self.*

The Holy Qur'an significantly reveals and pinpoints various aspects of human personality development. Identifying the negative tendencies of human nature is meant to emphasize the positive aspects that lead to the excellent flowering of the human personality.

Even where the *self* has been described as a *commander of evil* (أَمَّارَةٌ بِالسُّوءِ, 12:53), the contextual inference is to the effect that human *self* is capable of inviting evil (داعية بالسوء). This distinction is important in that human beings are made aware of their predominantly raw instinctiveness which, unless refined and trained, is naturally forceful enough to overwhelm any humanely cultivated qualities conducive to spiritual enhancement. This seems to be an aspect yet to be fully identified by modern psychologists.

Nevertheless, it is widely accepted today that emotional disorders can occasionally lead to mental illness. This can happen in some mysterious and arbitrary manner, in which the faculty of conscious perception is not involved. Consequently, the mind functions in an aberrant manner, so as to carry out the dictates or impulses of emotional origin.

The positive and negative factors in human personality development are further examined in subsequent sections, in the context of modernistic sexual permissiveness. Meanwhile, the meaning and connotation of suppressing carnality should be explained.

Islam does not support suppressing human desires in any way. This is true for other instincts, too. Then, what is meant by suppression of carnal desire? Does it mean eliminating the causes leading to it?

In the Islamic context, it signifies effective and moderate coping with the human lusts. This is emphasized also in many scholarly explanations of Islamic morality. Islam teaches human beings to have the sensibility of the mind rule over the sensuality of the body. An individual must not be led by his natural instincts (نفس امارة); rather, he must manage them wholesomely. As mentioned earlier, Islam does not preach ascetic suppression of the natural desires.

When people are commanded by their instincts, they exhibit personality disorders, and their consciousnesses are disrupted. In order to keep the instincts from swaying the conscience, the natural outpourings of the carnal desires must be pacified, or else offset to prevent temptation, emotional disorders, or promiscuity.

Of course, the animalistic instincts must be tamed in order to eliminate temptation. This is possible when temptation is avoided in a natural and harmonious manner. This necessitates overcoming tendencies leading to social evils and psychological ills. Thus, eliminating temptation does not require casting out the external forces, human or otherwise, which may be causing it.

On the contrary, the internal causes and tendencies must be eliminated. This is necessary to avoid the malignant development of the libido. Vulnerability to any undesirable external influences is also overcome in the process. A wholesome development of human instincts is a process requiring either a salutary compliance or a moral inhibition of their negative upsurge depending on their nature and content.

Incidentally, it is notable that the phrase *killing the carnal desire* does not occur in any specific teaching of Islam. Any reference to it is only by way of explaining the need for healthy personality growth.

Towards satisfying natural instincts and desires, any one-sided approach entails shortcomings, which are not often removable subsequently. Since the last century, sex-oriented psychological research achievements concentrated on proving that suppression of the natural instincts and desires was fraught with many adverse consequences to individuals. These findings proved to be valuable.

For one thing, the traditional thinking which said that, the more the baser instincts are suppressed, the greater the scope for enhancing the higher faculties (such as the intellectual) has been invalidated. There is growing realization that suppressed or unsatisfied instincts and desires have consequences for the individual and society, and these consequences are often hidden from the conscious mind.

The question of satisfying carnal instincts and spontaneous desires could well be left to one's own judgment. For only the human intellect can prevent any untoward instinctive development. One can purposefully manage one's own natural promptings and ensure that they are not negated or harmed or frustrated in an unwholesome manner.

Many nervous and mental disorders affecting individuals,

and even society as a whole, have been traced by psychologists and psychiatrists to personal feelings of deprivation, especially sexual deprivation. They have proved that emotional deprivation give rise to psychological complexes. The psychological afflictions can assume even dangerous proportions, resulting in sadism, morbid insolence, extreme jealousy, reclusiveness, cynicism, and so on.

These findings concerning human instincts and desires represent some of the psychologically significant discoveries and successes achieved by mankind.

An increasingly popular awareness of an interest in the nature and content of the human senses may lead to further research and findings. The discoveries are likely to be of a kind that conforms to the needs of technological and industrial progress. These may be conducive to better identification and greater employment of the natural, especially inorganic, forces. However, psychological and spiritual aspects of problems may not receive popular attention. Thus, their awareness may be confined to the learned and the wise.

Psychosomatic integrity in human personality development has been emphasized since the beginning of recorded history. Islam, too, has significantly pinpointed its need. Traditional moralists, as well as behavioural scientists, have always tried to reflect the cumulative knowledge and wisdom evolved in the past in one way or the other. Nevertheless, the fact remains that the psychosomatic approach has been scientifically established only during the last one hundred years or so.

Now, let us see how best the principle of psychosomatic wellbeing can be practised. Evidently, it cannot be used as easily as penicillin. It is an abstraction that requires a certain ability to comprehend. Moreover, it is suggestive of the intricacy and diversity of psychological and other problems, which often have been investigated in a microscopic perspective. At the same time, obscuring moral considerations and underrating personal character development have come to be the order of the day, which apparently suits many ease-loving and hard-pressed people of modern societies.

Worse still, the genuine need to promote wholesome and innocuous fulfilment of natural instincts and desires has been misinterpreted or misapplied in actual practice. Instead, an unrestrained gratification of human sexuality has come to be prescribed, ostensibly for avoiding their undesirable frustration. Consequently, psychological complexes and tensions have increased rather than decreased.

Statistics often indicate a virulent growth of psychological diseases, mental disorders, suicide, crimes of passion, anxiety, mental anguish, restlessness, hopelessness, pessimism, jealousy, malice, malevolence and similar other psychosomatic manifestations of unwholesome human personality development. The inhumane development of an ever-increasing number of individuals has been explained to be arising from the modernistic permissiveness with regard to natural instincts and desires, including uninhibited or unrestrained sex.

For centuries there has been widespread and insistent opposition to any permissiveness towards lust and sensuality. This was mainly in order to avoid the baneful effects of human sensuality or deviation on individual morality, spirituality and activities, as well as on the peace and integrity of society. All this has been reversed in a sudden and arbitrary manner by the protagonists of a modernistic permissive society.

The reversal was sought on the grounds that eschewing lust and subjecting oneself to chastity, rectitude, endurance, moral and social restrictions or limits disturbs a person's spiritual wellbeing and his own society's peacefulness. Above all, the reversal was sought as if morality and avoidance of lust or sensuality are actually irrelevant to any benign personal conduct, or a positive development of human personality.

This about-face has come about as if there has always been a great and insistent demand to lift moral restraints or limits. The social change was sought as if it were really necessary to absolve people of their moral scruples, duties and obligations and thus liberating them from an assumed malevolence.

The reformists seem to have been motivated by some imaginary need to let people enjoy themselves to their heart's content, irrespective of any moral compunctions or conscious commitment to chastity and rectitude. All these are supposed to be conducive towards peacefully maintaining whatever social order has come to prevail, while purporting to free the people from psychological disorders!

Evidently, the seductive concept of allowing natural instincts and desires free reign has been offered as a reformatory safeguard against moral and social constraints, as if these are corrupting! Furthermore, this concept has readily appealed to many young and single persons, including a substantial number in our own country.

From what we have noticed, the supporters of a permissive society have a peculiar way of thinking. They seem to believe that nothing is better for people than placing themselves at the disposal of the sweet dictates of their hearts, while allowing their hearts to be dominated even by lust.

At the same time, they apparently rationalize that the actions resulting from their way of thinking can be construed as both human and moralistic to the point of their being accepted as potential experts in sophisticated social behaviour. They apparently suggest that their thinking augurs them well, even if it represents a subject of ridicule to others. Furthermore, they profess to seek both self-gratification and service to their kind. They mean to ensure satiation of every bodily urge and to cope with any spiritual need, as well.

In other words, they seem to equate good or normal

conduct with sensuality. Their imagination is not totally dissimilar to the metaphorical use of love by some mystics, in the manner of Sufis. They apparently sought communion with whatever images of female beauty and love they could visualize, even in Divine terms!

Consequently, the modernistic free reign of the natural instincts and desires failed to cure psychosomatic illnesses or neurotic disorders or induce spiritual contentment. Human afflictions continue to spread, bringing one misfortune after another in an increasingly pernicious manner. No wonder, some promoters of uninhibited sexual development, such as Freud, were sensible enough to retract – or at least modify or clarify – their original claims.

They reiterated that there was no easy way out of the traditionally evolved social norms and constraints. They clarified that human sexual lusts are not a programmable quantity, or a self-contained input, which can be completely or instantly satisfied. They also referred to the need to sublimate these desires, so as to channel human energies directly towards intellectual enhancement to solve educational, scientific, cultural, socio-economic and technological problems.

New morals like Bertrand Russell's are supposed to be conducive to a positive development of human personality. At the same time, it is alleged that traditional morals inhibit human development. The fact that, in the wake of the new morals, human afflictions and distress have become aggravated disproves the abovementioned claims, so that they deserve to be subjected to the same allegations they make against traditional morals.

Today, social scientists are endeavouring to cope with the resulting manifestations and difficulties in their societies. Young persons are consciously avoiding marriage. Pregnancy and upbringing of children are becoming somewhat abhorrent to many women, who seem to be even less interested in housekeeping.

Marriages are more evident in traditional societies and conservative families than in modern ones. On the other hand, neurotic conflicts in both sexes are increasing, evidencing unusual psychosomatic and spiritual ailments.

Some social scientists hold that traditional social values have been fundamentally overtaken and superseded by the manpower requirements of the modern industrial revolution. However, morals – traditional or otherwise – should actually retain their intrinsic values and connotations. They are not affected by any changing patterns of human living or a shift from an agricultural to an industrial society.

Changes in any familiar patterns of human living and social interaction are only construed to be fundamental in some revolutionary intellectual way! The seemingly revolutionary thinking is attributable to some individuals with whom must lie the grave responsibility for any consequent misfortunes befalling humanity.

Even Bertrand Russell speaks of the pitfalls involved in speculative thinking, including his own. For instance, he favours an unrestrained gratification of the sexual instinct on one hand, and concedes the necessity of adhering to a time-tested system of its self-regulation, on the other. However, it is not intended to elaborate further on the pros and cons of modernistic thinking concerning human sexuality.

In reality, fulfilling the natural instincts appropriately – instead of suppressing them – is not the same as liberating sexuality by denouncing the age old moral restraints and constraints. The natural instincts and desires are not incompatible with chastity and virtue. In fact, they are adequately satisfied only within a chaste and virtuous regulatory framework, which avoids the evils of promiscuity, enforced celibacy or self-denial and the resultant emotional disturbances.

In other words, an appropriate nurturing of human instincts means nothing other than overcoming lust and baser inclinations. The basic distinction between human beings and animals is that humans are capable of two kinds of desires: one is a genuinely natural urge and the other is a pseudo-desire.

Genuine desires conform to the naturally essential requirements, such as the desires for food, survival, self-protection, the sexual drive, the inclination for aggression or domination and so on. Each of the genuinely natural desires has a specific function. However, aside from serving specific purposes, they are also each capable of forming a basis for a pseudo-desire, such as the well-known false appetite.

Most natural desires are amenable to complete satisfaction. Satisfying the others, including the sexual drive, involves psychological complications. For the mind and the human spirit are at times capable of sustaining bodily desires beyond the natural limits of physiological satisfaction. Some intellectually sustained cravings never reach a saturation point!

Accordingly, it is quite misleading to suggest an uninhibited gratification of carnal desires, by prescribing freedom from moral restraints and curbs on the natural instincts. Those who prescribe it fail to distinguish between the qualities of human beings and animals. They ignore the fact that there can be no end to human desire or craving.

Human beings are prone to seize every opportunity towards self satisfaction. They unceasingly avail every occasion to advance their own interests. This is equally true in matters of acquiring wealth, economics, politics and government, as well as in seeking to dominate others or to intensify sexuality.

To suggest that relieving the sex urge is like attending to one's call of nature, such as urination or defecation, is quite misleading, too. Any question of evacuating from one's self his or her own moral scruples or conditions, in the process of obtaining instant sexual relief, does not arise. Conversely, safeguarding one's morality cannot mean the same as accumulating urine. For, unlike moral continence, retention of urine is bound to cause bodily discomfort and disease.

For a better appreciation of the above point, let us assume that a person finds, along the avenues and streets he frequents, several clean, well-kept and even cost-free public urinals. Yet, one could not use them to his or her heart's content to an extent beyond what one's bladder permits! Accordingly, these nice urinals could not (or should not) unduly attract a person to urinate.

Some modernistic people assume that all human inclinations, even if they concern sex, aggression, domination or greed, should be freely allowed to be satisfied. This is supposed to result in the elimination of human deprivation, frustration or dissatisfaction in the process of satisfying one's desires. Their reasoning is based on a false assumption. For, as pointed out earlier, complete gratification of all human desires is not possible.

Unlike in the case of animals, the human capacity to seek gratification of natural and acquired desires is not instinctively limited. Otherwise, there would have been no need for any human regulation of not only the sexual intercourse, but socio-economic and political interactions, as well. Even moral restraints would have been unnecessary where natural constraints made it impossible for anyone to seek excessive satisfaction or indulge in excesses. The very limitation of natural capacity to commit excesses would have served the purpose, as in the case of animals.

However, ethical limits and procedural regulations are necessary to promote just practices and fair transactions in the socio-economic and political fields.

Likewise the limitation and regulation of sexual behaviour and related activities, consistent with the needs of chastity and rectitude, should also be acceptable to everyone.

6

Love, Sexual Discipline and Chastity

Democratic Morality and Love in Personality Growth

The principles of human liberty and democracy should also govern morals, just as in the case of politics. Human beings should cope with their inborn instincts and natural desires in the same way as a just and democratic government does in respect to the masses of people.

Islam treats questions concerning sexual behaviour on the same ethical basis as is commonly recognized today in the regulation of political and economic activities. For individuals are prone to making genuine and willful mistakes in ordering their sexual lives on the basis of their own moral judgment. They may mistakenly or wantonly ignore the need to maintain a democratic concern for morality, in coping with their individual problems which arising from a lack of personal restraint and overall chaos.

In principle, any societal regulation of political and economic activities ought to recognize the relevant human instincts and tendencies. For, the aggressive instinct and tendency to dominate others can be instrumental in politics. Economic activities may be prompted by a desire to accumulate wealth. Likewise, sexual aptitude can lead to indulgence in lustful activities. However, it is not known why the supporters of the proposed new sexual freedom deem a laissez faire policy fit for sexual affairs only, while they seemingly accept that political and economic activities should be controlled.

One of the important aspects of sexual ethics concerns the emotion of love. Since ancient times, the essence of love has been given special attention in philosophy. The Islamic philosopher Ibn Sina wrote a treatise on love. Human love has been commonly acknowledged as a wholesome reality in terms of its all-embracing and sublime nature. In literature, especially poetry, love has not only been proudly eulogised (to the extent of proclaiming the superiority of the heart over the mind), but also contrasted with lust's debasingly animal-like nature.

Mostly in our literature we find that love has been extolled not only in terms of its Divine connotation, but even in its down-to-earth human emotional context. In either case, there has been no confusion of love with any kind of lust.

In contrast, there have been others, who chose to equate love with a sort of libido, or any persistent metabolic intensity of the sexual instinct. Evidently, they tended to assume that love is rather incapable of sublimation even in Divine terms. They treat love as if it has neither any spiritual origin, nor is it (or should it be) humane in quality, nor can it be humanitarian in purpose.

Those who treat love as both Divine and human differentiate between the animal-like manifestation and the humane accomplishment of love. The others make no such distinction, so that love and lust become synonymous.

Today, a third category of thinkers has become evident. They believe that all kinds of love are sexually prompted, but gradually the carnal motivation assumes a spiritual or contemplative aspect under specific conditions. To them, love is primarily sexual, with only occasional platonic manifestations. However, this dual or two-fold quality of love is affirmed by them only in terms of its expression, objective and effects. There is no duality in so far as the origin and causation of love are concerned.

With regard to the last category of thinkers mentioned above, it is not a matter of surprise that they believe in a material basis of human spirituality They see no insurmountable difficulty in the mutual transformation of the material and spiritual aspects of human behaviour. In fact, one of them claims that every spiritual affair has a natural basis and every natural thing has a spiritual extension.[1]

Be that as it may, we need not discuss the above in any great psychological and philosophical depth. We can thus avoid going into the pros and cons of the many ancient and current interpretations of any basis of love. For the time being, it should be enough to suggest that love, in effect, can bring about creativity of the human intellect and spirit, as well as induce artistic and cultural refinements of sociological importance.

The above suggestion is valid, irrespective of whether or not love originates in the sexual instinct, and then becomes capable of expressing itself in physical and also spiritual terms, in an interchangeable manner. Any sublime effect of love is far different from its alleged instinctiveness, or simple animal-like lustfulness, which seeks no more than its physiological gratification.

Love does sometimes evidence itself as lust. When lust overtakes human beings, humans become self-centred, regarding love as a mere tool or means of self gratification. However, when human beings evidence love as a genuine affection, they are no longer self-centred. On the contrary, their love signifies the most desirable spirit of self-sacrifice.

In other words, individuals in genuine love are capable of overcoming their self-centred motivations for the sake of each other.

World literature is replete with love's many-splendored qualities, including those of a catalyst, teacher and inspirer. From Persian literature, we may quote a verse from Sa'di:

هر کس که عشق اندر او کمند انداخت

بمراد ویش بباید ساخت

هر که عاشق نگشت مرد نشد

نقره فائق نگشت تا نگداخت

Whoever falls in love beyond himself
Yields to love but his own self.
Whoever loved not, evolved not manfulness;
Silver unmelted gives not brightfulness.

Another famous Iranian poet, Hafiz, refers to a nightingale's love of roses and muses as follows:

بلبل از فیض گل آموخت سخن، ورنه نبود

این همه قول وغزل، تعبیه در منقارش

By the rose's grace, nightingales do their singing
All those songs and lyrics so pleasing
Beyond what their beaks do improvising!

No doubt, love has been eulogised in many ways, both in the East and West. Yet, there has come to be a difference between the Eastern and Western conceptualizations of love. To many Westerners, love can be worthwhile as long as it embodies the sweetness mutually attainable by lovers. Individuals of the opposite sex in the West prefer the desirability and enjoyability of living together in mutual love and comfort to the constant annoyance and boredom of living as singles. They aim at maximizing their enjoyment of life.

In the East, love is regarded as something inexorably desirable in itself, for it lends an overall perspective to the human personality while ennobling and inspiring the spirit. No wonder love has been described as a catalyst, a purifier, and so on. Evidently, in all these and other attributes, one can hardly discern any implicit suggestion to the effect that love is no more than an introduction to the sweet union that usually follows it, or to mere feelings of enjoying living together in body and spirit.

Even to some impressionable Easterners, love between prospective spouses may signify something preliminary to their subsequent pleasures of union and living together only.

However, even their preliminary experience of being loved by each other can (or ought to) progressively enhance their humaneness. This is not like its becoming something merely conducive to any anticipation of enjoyments from conjugal relations or cohabitation.

In either case, if love is construed as a real introduction to union of man and woman, in terms of becoming one in body and spirit, this is all the more conducive to the wholesomeness of human achievement.

In short, in love, as in several other matters, Westerners and Easterners differ in their intellectual approach. A typical Westerner is often unable to nurture love within any abstract framework that goes beyond any mechanical process of coping with problems of routine living. Eventually, he comes round to distinguishing love from lust, and also to believing in empathy and spiritual harmony, which it is capable of breeding.

Otherwise, love comes to him as a handy natural talent, leading to marriage or cohabitation, according to the social requirements of living. On the other hand, a typical Easterner seeks to cherish love beyond the requirements of routine living.

Had love been sexual in origin, quality and effect, it would probably not have necessitated separate treatment in sexual ethics. Whatever was discussed earlier concerning the pros and cons of sexual ethics would have been rather sufficient. However, love's origin or, at any rate, its psychological quality and social effects can be quite safely construed as being independent of the sexual instinct.

Accordingly, morals concerning the nurturing of human inclination to love can be treated in a manner distinguishable from that of the sexual instinct. Gratifying the sexual instinct is not the only concomitant of love. For sexual gratification is not enough to sustain love, which needs psychological contentment, too. Moreover, any denial of love can possibly lead to afflictions, which cannot be remedied by any animal-like gratification of the sexual instinct, assuming that the former is derived from the latter.

Bertrand Russell endorses the need for profound love as follows:

> Those who have never known the deep intimacy and the intense companionship of happy mutual love have missed the best thing that life has to give; unconsciously, if not consciously, they feel this and the resulting disappointment inclines them towards envy, oppression and cruelty.[2]

Sometimes, it is claimed that religion is love's enemy. The usual reasoning behind the claim is based on a situation where a religion fails to distinguish between love and lust. Thus, the wickedness of lust is ascribed to love, as well. The allegation is not true in the case of Islam.

Yet, it can be relevant to Christianity. Islam does not treat sexual passion as wicked in itself, nor does it consider love as something bad or undesirable.

Deeply sincere and mutual love between spouses is highly respected in Islam. Islamic teachings commend realization of love on a sound and lasting basis.

In the general context of religion versus love, there is one point that is often overlooked. This concerns the tendency for mutual opposition between human intellect and love. Some moralists have wrongly overlooked this in indiscriminately excluding love from morality. They only regarded love as blind and capable of overruling the intellect. They believed that love is not amenable to reason, inferring wrongly that it is also least susceptible to conventional legal or moral disciplining. In other words, they saw love as nothing but anarchic exuberance and rebelliousness.

Accordingly, religions or social systems, which based their morality on intellectual considerations alone, were not conducive to any salutary treatment of love. They treated love as something beyond the scope of any recommendation or advice. This is notwithstanding that, regarding love, the most necessary advice concerns one's response to any casual manifestation of love in extenuating circumstances over which one is supposed to have no control. This is in order to maximize the sublime and beneficial effects of love, while remaining immune to its harmful consequences, if any.

In the above context, the main question that arises concerns the mutually inclusive relationship of love and chastity. One may ask whether or not love can, in its most positive sense, flourish in any permissive social environments. Or, is it simply a question of whether or not love's meaningfulness is invariably linked with any social preference for chastity, envisaging a certain prosaic status for women?

In his book *The Pleasures of Philosophy,* Will Durant acknowledged that love was generally agreed to be the most fascinating thing in the course of human life. At the same time, he noted with surprise that very rarely attention was focused on the origin and growth of love, in the relevant multilingual, poetic and philosophical works of most sensational poets and writers on the subject of love.

Will Durant further pointed out that the analytical part of literary and scientific material concerning love was extremely limited. Typical coverage ranged from the ordinary reproduction of protozoa to the self-sacrificing spirit of Dante, or the poetic ecstasies of Petrarch among similar others. In all these efforts, any thorough investigation of the astonishing factuality, the natural origin, the factors in wholesome evolutionary growth and similar other aspects of love were found by him to be missing.

Earlier herein, we have identified three distinct schools of ancient and modern thought concerning the origin and purpose of love, so as to deduce its unique or two-sided interaction with the sexual instinct. We have noted that love, as conceived in both the West and the East, is distinct from lust. Also, it is universally recognised as praiseworthy and respectable, although the relevant conceptualizations differ, as already explained. What remains to be examined now is mainly the question of love in relation to chastity, especially in order to specify the areas and conditions in which they can flourish.

With regard to love and chastity, the relevant social regulations can be either explicit or implicit in moral terms. Where these are explicitly regulated, women may be assigned an elevated position in society, so that they are ordinarily not approachable by men. In the other situation, where love and chastity are implicitly promoted, but not regulated, women's position is subject to the utter tedium of placing themselves at the disposal and protection of their men. One may wonder as to which one of these two sets of conditions are apt to enhance love and chastity.

Incidentally, it is notable that the so-called open or permissive societies are innately incapable of promoting conditions for any deep and intense love relationships. Their conditions lead to waywardness and wantonness, transient affairs, and momentary and lustful pleasures. No wonder, women's position in these so-called free environments continues to be rather prosaic, while both men and women remain liable to miss heartfelt and genuine mutual love and responsiveness.

Permissive social environments further sensuality and licentiousness. They are not conducive to the beneficial love held in esteem by philosophers and sociologists, in terms of its intensely evolved, deeply responsive and unselfish effects. Given appropriate social conditions, love can indeed enable personalities mellowed by it to concentrate individual energies for good purposes, render their perceptions clear and keen, induce empathy towards the beloved, as well as promote genius-like originality and excellence of thoughts and achievements.

Genuine love's wholesome qualities have been commended not only by the ancients, but also by modern writers, including some who favoured the proposed new sexual freedom. In his magnum opus, *The History of Civilization*, Will Durant discusses both the male homosexual connotation of the traditional Greek depiction of love in their ballads and the heterosexual love episodes of the *A Thousand and One Nights* fame, dating back to centuries earlier than the Middle Ages. He indicated that interest in the oriental stories of natural love grew to an extent more than that of the routine exhortations of the Church towards promoting chastity and virtue.

Furthermore, Will Durant regarded a literary compilation, such as *A Thousand and One Nights*, as a possible source of inspiration for the subsequent lyrical compositions abroad. He referred to one usually sarcastic contemporary Western writer's extraordinary remark to the effect that love meant the same to human carnality as life signified to human spirituality.

Indeed, as observed by Will Durant, many began to wonder how the abstraction of human sensuality into the most sensible love can be explained. People became curious about the intellectual and similar other factors that transform an animal-like instinctive hunger, such as evidenced at times by the human lusts, into serene and tender love. The curiosity revolved around the point as to how the carnal passion might become spiritual compassion.

Will Durant further probed into an introspective sublimation of carnal desires and the consequent platonic imaginings about a beloved in various intellectual contexts. He raised the question as to whether or not the aforesaid sublimation was the outcome of the growth of civilization, involving progressively late marriages!

He apparently believed that an answer to the question he posed might lie in a human tendency. He pointed out that whatever one sought and did not find became dear and extraordinarily valuable. Thus, appreciation of beauty could vary with the intensity of desire. And, desire would intensify when inhibited and diminish when sated.

Will Durant referred to William James' contention that female modesty was not instinctive, but rather inculcated by successive generations of women, out of fear that any other behaviour would attract undesirable interest or contempt of others. He pointed out that shameless women could not be of any sustained interest to men. Only women who refrained from any exuberant gaiety and who abstained from either inviting or conceding male attention succeeded in attracting men.

According to Will Durant, any exposure of the intimate parts of the human body from their normal state of concealment might not evoke more than casual interest on the part of viewers. In any case, it would seldom lead to any instant arousal of carnal desire. For even young men prefer modesty in young women. In doing so, they might not necessarily comprehend that the delicateness of female reserve could be indicative of a high degree of tactful reaction, as well as tenderness.

Furthermore, modesty in women might be capable of endearing them to men and awakening mutual love, in anticipation of any subsequent consummation. Thus, men could be prompted to enhance their capabilities and resolution towards significant achievements, by drawing on their otherwise dormant life-oriented energies.

At the same time, Will Durant mentioned that modern young women seem only too willing to discard conventional morality, as if it were some old clothes that went out of fashion. He observed that these women could be audacious not only in displaying themselves, but in their sartorial tastes. Consequently, diminished masculine imaginability concerning female appeal was specified by him to be the only adverse effect of the radical change in the women's outlook and behaviour. He opined that, had it not been for men's residual imaginability, perhaps there would have remained no visualization of female beauty.

As for Bertrand Russell's romantic love, we may quote his

own words as follows:

> The essential of romantic love is that it regards the beloved object as very difficult to possess and as very precious . . . The belief in the immense value of the lady is a psychological effect of the difficulty of obtaining her, and I think it may be laid down that when a man has no difficulty in obtaining a woman, his feeling towards her does not take the form of romantic love.[3]

Then, Bertrand Russell says:

> From the point of view of the arts, it is certainly regrettable when women are too accessible; what is most to be desired is that they should be difficult but not impossible to access . . . In a state of complete freedom, on the other hand, a man capable of great love poetry is likely to have so much success through his charm that he will seldom have need of his best imaginative efforts in order to achieve a conquest.[4]

Furthermore, he mentions in another context as follows:

> Among modern emancipated people, love in the serious sense with which we are concerned is suffering a new danger. When people no longer feel any moral barrier against sexual intercourse on every occasion when even a trivial impulse inclines to it, they get into the habit of dissociating sex from serious emotion and from feelings of affection; they may even come to associate it with feelings of hatred.[5]

Notes

[1] Will Durant, *The Pleasures of Philosophy* (New York: Simon and Schuster, Inc., 1953).

[2] Bertrand Russell, *Marriage and Morals*, 84.

[3] Ibid., 49.

[4] Ibid., 53-54.

[5] Ibid., 38.

7

Concluding Remarks

How strange that Bertrand Russell deemed it fit to emphasize the need for love in the serious sense, almost in a moralist vein! His proposed new sexual freedom has not been fully clarified. For he judged chastity and virtue to be dispensable for all sexual purposes. He construed marriage to be in no way obstructive to free sexual love. He implicitly recommended free sexual relations even with persons other than legal spouses, provided legitimacy of conception is ensured. In short, he approved of all kinds of non-violent and harmless sexual relations. All these he advocated seemingly because he found no reason to uphold conventional sexual morality, except for comparing and coordinating one's private and public interests.

With his extreme thinking, as indicated above, Bertrand Russell could not have been expected to project any correct image of morals, which would seek to regulate human sexuality, in order to nurture it on the basis of tender feelings of love and affection. In any case, it is very clear that Bertrand Russell and others like him have sought to introduce a kind of communal sexuality. Societies where free sexual love prevails can hardly promote any genuine love.

At any rate, in the permissive societies, love would not retain the same meaning given to it by philosophers of old. We may recall that love has been represented as the zenith of one's life and of one's enthusiasm for living – a teacher, trainer, inspirer and a catalyst. In fact, people who spend their entire lives without the benefit of love remain unfortunate enough not to deserve to be called human.

In the above context, two essential points are notable. The first one concerns the position that love, from the points of view of quality and purpose, is distinct from animal concupiscence and sexual lust. Moreover, it belongs to the realm of spirituality, an aspect which is incompatible with the principles of materialism. Yet, it is acceptable to one who ponders over spiritual matters even in what would appear to be a materialistic perspective. This much is admitted by Bertrand Russell himself when he says that 'love is something far more than desire for sexual intercourse.'[1]

Furthermore, Bertrand Russell recognizes love and (ironically enough) sexual morality when he says:

> Love has its own proper ideals and its own intrinsic moral standards. These are obscure both in Christian teaching and in the indiscriminate revolt against all sexual morality which has sprung up among considerable sections of the young generations.[2]

The second point elaborates on the spiritual aspect of love. Spirituality of love is evidenced in two stages. At the outset, it is indicated by a state of love in which emotional restiveness and intensity develop in the absence of the beloved. Subsequently, it manifests itself in sustained agitation of individual spirit. This leads to intellectual concentration and to prevalence of chastity and virtue in the spirit of the lover, so that occasionally geniuses are produced. In either case, the human spirit undergoes great changes.

However the aforementioned great transformations of human spirit are possible only in a situation where lovers remain separated and/or their love remains unrequited. No sublime achievements are likely in a situation where lovers do not miss each other. At any rate, in the latter case, even passionate love may not reach the very height of its potential intensity in order to achieve the significant qualities noted by philosophers.

A person becomes capable of manifesting great love from within himself or herself. Then, the spirit becomes agitated and seeks rest in the person or in the image of the beloved.

The image may be construed even beyond its real counterpart. Thus, eventually, the former assumes greater significance to its accustomed lover than that of the real person of the distant beloved.

Where lovers remain united, mutual affection and kindness, as well as sincerity and repose, may be evidenced by them. A soundly endeavouring married couple will take the trials of life in their stride. Their combined abilities to do so can well be enhanced by their spiritual or intellectual compatibility, too. At the same time, they should be able to keep up their moral integrity, if their society is corrupt and polluted. In other words, they should not be tempted by any prospects of free sexual love offered by their society.

Spouses who are able to continually uphold chastity and virtue do so primarily by confining their sexual enjoyments to their conjugal rights. Then, in old age when sexual passions subside, they can keep up their mutual affection through carefully nurtured and established chaste and virtuous companionship. Couples bound by sexual interests alone cannot be expected to evolve a well-integrated family living pattern and a lasting companionship.

A wife's entitlement to alimony and to sharing her husband's wealth represent the most significant economic and financial provisions instituted for marriage and family living. These are in consideration of the exclusiveness of the spouses' conjugal relationship. The genuine interaction between a couple, which is expected in marriage and family living, is envisaged in terms of their individual and collective endeavours as well as in the broader context of appropriately maintaining their social environment.

Mutual affection and sincerity, as well as humane compassion and tenderness, are highly desirable attributes in married couples, in the context of their mutual and social interactions. These are often evidenced in societies governed by Islamic moral and legal checks and balances. In others, such as those in the West, these qualities are seldom noticeable.

In the case of separated lovers, the afflicted individual spirits are likely to become all the more sensitive and poignant. They soar and delve, as well as keep attracting and getting attracted. In the other case of united lovers, who evidence mutually affectionate enjoyment and deep sincerity, their marital union itself will be capable of producing significant attainments. One may be rather skeptical about the former. However, with regard to the latter, one is more likely to agree.

The Divine creation of the female counterpart of man emphasized their companionship and mutual affection. This is made clear in the Glorious Qur'an, as follows:

وَمِنْ آيَاتِهِ أَنْ خَلَقَ لَكُم مِّنْ أَنفُسِكُمْ أَزْوَاجًا لِّتَسْكُنُوا إِلَيْهَا وَجَعَلَ بَيْنَكُم مَّوَدَّةً وَرَحْمَةً

And from among His signs is that He created spouses
from your selves, so that you might find rest in them,
and he instilled love and graciousness between you
(30:21).

The above passage contains two keywords, which are indicative of the Divine intention in creating the human pair. These keywords are: love and graciousness. Their significance is very clear that God did not merely create woman as mate for man, but indicated also that the pairing had envisaged inculcation of the abovementioned humane qualities.

It is needless to add that the above humane qualities are indeed far different from those of human sensuality, or libido, as interpreted by some modernistic societies.

Rumi reflected the above point in his stanza:

زین للناس حق آراسته است

ز آنچه حق آراست کی تانند رست

چون پی یسکن الیهاش آفرید

کی تواند آدم از حوا برید

آنچنین خاصیّتی در آدمی است

مهر، حیوان را کم است، آن از کمی است

مهر ورقت وصف انسانی بود

خشم وشهوت وصف حیوانی بود

> The World owes to God its loveliness,
> That which He forms retains its exquisiteness,
> Since He made it as Man's abode,
> How Adam's love for Eve can erode?
> That is how it is with Mankind
> Humane love is ordained not for animal-kind
> For, pure love and compassion are to Mankind
> What aggravation and lust are to animal-kind.[3]

According to Will Durant, love attains perfection when it is sustained through old age. Then, it will provide a cushioning effect during the loneliness of senility and the approach of death. His view confirms the fact that love extends far beyond libido, in that anyone relying on the latter does so in vain and rather superficially on the basis of the sexual instinct alone.

In fact, Will Durant believed that the spirit of love could survive beyond the last trace of human physiological fitness. In senility, loving hearts retain their fresh spiritual excellence, while the emotional needs of the body are perfectly fulfilled on a continuing basis.

To sum up, love assumes significance when its intrinsically humane qualities are nurtured and evidenced. Any separation of lovers accentuates – rather than falsifies – the blossoming of love that is attained with chastity and rectitude on the part of lovers.

Genuine love is unlikely to flourish in sexually and secularly permissive societies. They do not provide the necessary conditions for promoting the same, even in any romantic or poetic contexts. An average married couple in a modernistic society lacks an overall perspective, such as that of Islam, and so they remain unable to attain a deeply unifying and sincere love relationship.

Notes

[1]   Bertrand Russell, *Marriage and Morals*, 83.
[2]   Ibid., 86-87.
[3]   Rumi, *Masnavi.*

Index